FRED FLINTSTONE'S ADVENTURES with PULLEYS

Work Smarter, Not Harder

by Mark Weakland

illustrated by Paco Sordo

Curious Fox
a capstone company-publishers for children

Yes, dear.

Pulleys help me to do work. A pulley is like a wheel and axle. A rope or cord wraps around a grooved wheel. When I pull, the rope rotates around the wheel and pulls up the blinds.

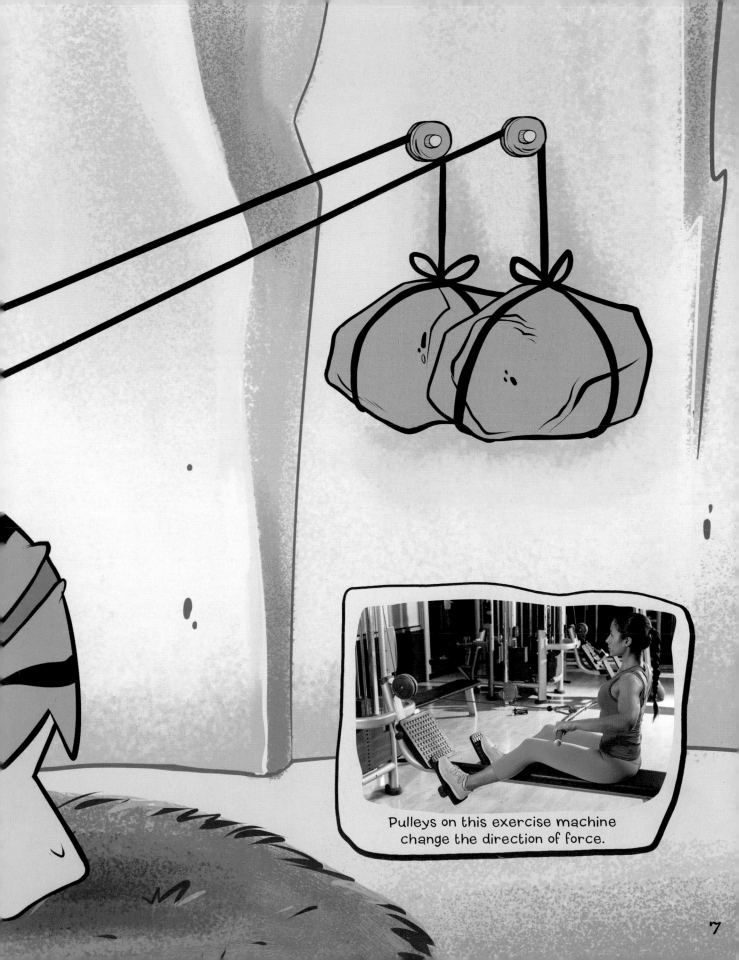

Pulleys on this exercise machine change the direction of force.

A pulley on a flagpole lets you raise and lower the flag.

Yabba-dabba-doo! When one pulley isn't enough, I use two. Using multiple pulleys makes work easier. The pulleys lessen the force needed to lift heavy things. If I use two pulleys, I can use half as much force to lift this heavy sail.

Hold on, Barney! You're working too hard. Step aside and let me show you how it's done.

A block and tackle uses pulleys to lift all types of heavy objects.

Aye, aye Fred.

Sometimes a block and tackle is best. It decreases the amount of force needed to lift a heavy object. The weight of the object is split equally between the two pulleys. I only have to use half as much force to lift the boat. Now that's the Fred Flintstone way!

BOAT MARINA

Pulleys and ropes allow rock climbers to defy gravity.

Glossary

abseil   slide down a strong rope

defy   resist

effort   force applied to a machine to do work

force   push or pull exerted upon an object

gravity   force that pulls objects together

inclined plane   sloping surface that is used to move objects to different levels

input force   initial force used to get a machine working

load   object that moves when a force is applied

multiple   involving many parts or many things

output force   (also called the load) weight of the object to be moved

pulley   grooved wheel turned by a rope, belt or chain that often moves heavy objects

reduce   make something smaller or less in amount or size

rotate   spin around

Read more

How Things Work (See Inside), Conrad Mason
(Usborne Publishing Ltd, 2009)

How Things Work Encyclopedia (First Reference), Dorling
Kindersley (DK Children, 2012)

Making Machines with Pulleys (Simple Machine Projects),
Chris Oxlade (Raintree, 2015)

Website

www.dkfindout.com/uk/science/simple-machines/
Find out more about how we use simple machines.

Index

Look for all the books in the series:

First published in 2016 by Curious Fox, an imprint of Capstone Global Library Limited, 264 Banbury Road, Oxford, OX2 7DY - Registered company number: 6695582

www.curious-fox.com

Illustrations by Paco Sordo
All characters in this publication are fictitious and any resemblance to real persons, living or dead, is purely coincidental.

Printed and bound in China.
ISBN 978 1 78202 382 1
20 19 18 17 16
10 9 8 7 6 5 4 3 2 1

Edited by Alesha Halvorson
Designed by Ashlee Suker
Picture Research by Tracy Cummins
Production by Kathy McColley
Creative Director: Nathan Gassman

A CIP catalogue for this book is available from the British Library.

Acknowledgements
Shutterstock: Shutterstock: Anna Omelchenko, 19, holbox, 7, JuliusKielaitis, 9, Volodymyr Kyrylyuk, 16

Thanks to our adviser for his expertise, research, and advice:
Paul Ohmann, PhD, Associate Professor of Physics
University of St. Thomas, St. Paul, Minnesota, USA.

Every effort has been made to contact copyright holders of material reproduced in this book. Any omissions will be rectified in subsequent printings if notice is given to the publisher.

All the Internet addresses (URLs) given in this book were valid at the time of going to press. However, due to the dynamic nature of the Internet, some addresses may have changed, or sites may have changed or ceased to exist since publication. While the author and publisher regret any inconvenience this may cause readers, no responsibility for any such changes can be accepted by either the author or publisher.